growing pains

Eliana Idzikowski

BookLeaf Publishing

India | USA | UK

Presentation by *BookLeaf Publishing*

Web: www.bookleafpub.com

E-mail: info@bookleafpub.com

ISBN: 9789360949907

First edition 2024

to my younger self

ACKNOWLEDGEMENT

To those who took the time to share their love with me.
Thank you for believing in me
I am forever grateful.

PREFACE

Within these poems, i present a journey of hurt, healing, and hope. A gentle reminder that life isn't linear but rather a winding path filled with bumps and surprises.

trapped

the worlds a little dark
and my mind is falling apart
but how do you tell them that you're broken
how do you reach out for hand that has just
opened
how can i call out for help
when i open my mouth and nothing comes out
and even if i did would anyone care

is there anyone there
who will wait for me
who sees what i see?

or am i just lost
am i just broken
swimming in sea that too deep
a sea full of tears
a sea full of my fears.

because every second of every moment my mind
begins to crumble with every person who walks
by
every smile on a face
echos in the back of my mind
but i can't seem to find
the person who wants to get out.

dreaming

i'm bursting at the seams
to float away into endless dreams
to live a life away from all
the pressure
the feelings
the madness

i just want to go
go away
go to a place where no one knows my face
go to a place where i cant leave a trace
somewhere where i can't hurt anyone
somewhere where i can just, run.
and run
and run
and it's not hard to look
through the darkness
through the clouds
because it's a place full of sunshine
a place to rest, a place to find
who i really am
without
the
madness.

for now, i'll sit in the darkness
and i'll try
and try
until one day i can reach the light

candlestick

i'm burning at both ends
trying my best to stay afloat
but with each passing second
I start to melt

to be one with the light
I always had the light
light for a room
light for another

but its when i'm alone
all I can see is darkness
near and far
theres no more light

left
for
me

nothing left to spare
just the dripping of wax
as i melt into a ball
the smell of smoke caresses my face

as i take a deep breath

and blow out the spark
that fuels the restless flame
constantly asking for more

but what is there left to give
when i have given my all
to the people
to the places

that just need a little bit of light.

night

there is comfort within my covers,
a shield of protection that blankets me in
security
there are things only my pillow knows
and yet i seem to think too much.

some nights i just want to sleep
and let my thoughts flow away
and yet they keep coming

i'm tired.
but sleep does not follow
as each action
each word
replays like a movie in front of me

tormenting the scared little girl inside.

metamorphisis

i'm terrified of change.

however, i long for change.
i yearn for change.

to be able to change the things
that feel engrained into my soul.
my habits,
my traits,
that just happens to push people away.

i like routine
i like schedules
i like normal

i dislike change

but i want to.

it's not always enough

i'm sorry

empty promise
empty phrase
empty words

they can mean something.
but only when paired with action do they matter.
action is hard
immobilizing

i try so hard.
often not enough
never enough to show the
guilt
or express my fault

i'm sorry my sorry was empty
i wish, it wasn't.
i wish i could've done better.

nightlight

there is a little light that illuminates my little
dark hole
it finds the small darkness i reside in,
and whispers little things to me

these little things make it
so warm
so cozy
so bright
in my dark little hole

and the more i listen,
the brighter it gets
no longer dark.

sometimes it flickers.
sometimes it needs a little light of its own
and i am strong enough to lend some of my light
as my fire has been ignited,
a spark nurtured to life
darkness no longer awaiting the nightlight

thank you amor for giving me my light back

rocks

authenticity thrives when there is nothing
no water, no sunlight, no air

just rocks.

stripped down to the soul
it roots deep within
without the impression of anything else
returning to just the bare rocks that lie within is
hard
but once one can find their rock or a reminder of
who they are
with no barriers,
no walls,
no expectations,
no outside influence,
it's easy to remember the roots
and the sprouts
and the flowers
that flourish from inside.

an ode to beauty

while easily defined Beauty is beyond words.
Beauty is vast or small or meek but spreads
everywhere.
Beauty can walk and talk and run
or trickle, grow, and learn.

she is often overlooked, formed in one way or
another
but if you reach deeper she is found
in every shape every size and always around.

she hides in the corner and sometimes you have
to look
It may be harder to find than just reading a book
sometimes she just likes to hide in nooks.

but we often don't see how Beauty
surrounds us, she is special and only just a little
mysterious in ways
the way she portrays

we often don't see Our Beauty.
but she's still there in times when we doubt
and though we can't find her every hour
the people around us can see our beautiful tower
inside and out, always here, overflowing with
the beauty we all have.

searching

digging
looking
learning
on the hunt
to find my people

because you gotta find your people
the ones who make you feel whole
it's hard to go it alone
not finding your people takes a toll

there is someone out there
waiting to be your person

once you find your people
you can find yourself

slow down

take a breath

in
and
out

look around
you're doing fine
there's no doubt

admiration comes in goes
watch how the water ebbs and flows
worries swirl like a storm
it's okay to let them fly away
gone with the wind

one breath more

in and out

waking up

i like to lay in bed
watch the sun stretch to the corners of my room
i like waiting for noon
i till i feel a spark of energy
big enough to get me up
i look to the sky
the stars
and the moon
throughout the day
each awaken in their own way

gratitude

three things i'm grateful for today
nature
my dog
you, for always believing in me

a reoccuring conversation

i don't know why it gets so hard sometimes
i don't know why i am the way that i am
i have so many questions so many things
awaiting an answer
i don't know when i'll change
i don't know if it will get any easier
and i hope not any harder
will i ever be the way i was?

it will get better
i promise

i don't feel better

you will just give it some time

senses

i like the way the wind whistles and the plants
bend back and forth
i like the smell of grass after a light rain
i like the sweet air that drifts from the flowers
so sweet you can taste it
i like the feeling of the sun's rays beaming down
after a cloud passes

spring changes to summer and summer to fall
fall falls into winter and it's back once more

the senses follow round and round, simple but
important
a reminder of where we've been and what is yet
to come

tick tock

18

in the sands of time, we rise and falter
through trials and tribulations, we learn to thrive
in every small step, we start to bloom
life can be relentless, but just give it some time
and soon you'll find your flower

home

through the storms and the rocks seas
the place we come to rest
is in the embrace of those we love best
for a home is not just bricks and stone
home is the person who makes us feel known

wandering

i am lost.
on a journey with no end in sight
i seek solace in the unknown
ready to take flight
to take a leap
that just might help me be found

sometimes

sometimes
sometimes i forget, a lot
sometimes i forget people exist.
sometimes i forget i have friends or people who
care about me.
sometimes i forget to take care of myself.
sometimes I just can't take care of myself.
sometimes i forget that i have things i have to
do.
sometimes i forget i have things to be excited
for, to learn, to discover. sometimes i forget
there are people counting on me, a world that's
larger than my confusing brain.
sometimes i can let go, and breathe.
i remember who i am and what i live for
i can be myself and not worry about all the
things i can't do, rather what i can
sometimes i forget i'm not alone in my journey.
sometimes i just want to be okay with being
alone.
sometimes i just can't get up.
sometimes i cry, sometimes i forget i can cry.
sometimes i just can't cry even though i want to
or need to

sometimes life is far too much a challenge to
remember how to live correctly. sometimes i
forget how to talk, or focus because there's too
much noise and i can't make it go quiet.
sometimes i'm too observant.
sometimes i'm not observant enough.

sometimes i remember i'm more than the lists i
create in my mind.
when i let go, i know that always

i can.

i can love, myself, the world around me, the
people around me, even with the weight i
continue to carry.

i can be me.

as simple as a smile

i love everyone i meet,
i love learning new things
i love nature
but i especially love love.

i love showing my people how much i care
through treats,
or cards,
hugs,
a simple smile,
notes,
reminders,
encouragement,

and in their joy, in their success and in their
pain,
i am there with them
remembering their love and warmth
the meaning they breathe into my life

the love they have for me,
and the love i share in return
they are my most prized possession,
my beautiful friends,
my chosen family,
my motivation to exist,
and why i keep trying each day to grow more.

a note to self

you can be loved.

there is enough love in the world to love you
all of you.

it's hard to learn how to love yourself.
especially when you forget.

somedays it's just hard to fathom how to love
yourself.

not being able to love yourself won't last forever.
i can promise that.

i promise it doesn't hinder your ability to love
others.
and it doesn't hinder your ability to try.

it is hard.
it will be hard.
but when you can push through
to see,
and hear,
and feel

the love that radiates throughout each and every
thing
you'll know once more

you are entirely capable.